# Stars Twinkle

and other questions
about space

Carole Stott

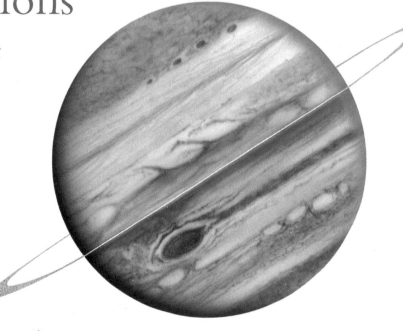

KINGFISHER

# KINGFISHER

Published 2011 by Kingfisher
an imprint of Macmillan Children's Books
a division of Macmillan Publishers Limited
20 New Wharf Road, London N1 9RR
Basingstoke and Oxford
Associated companies throughout the world
www.panmacmillan.com

First published 1995 by Kingfisher

Consultant: Dr David Hughes, Reader in Astronomy,
Sheffield University

ISBN 978-0-7534-3529-8
Copyright © Macmillan Children's Books 2011

9 8 7 6 5 4 3 2 1

1SPL/0212/WKT/UNTD/140MA

A CIP catalogue record for this book is available from
the British Library.

Printed in China

Illustrations: Chris Forsey cover, 4–5, 31; Ruby Green figure
artwork 19; Tony Kenyon (BL Kearley Ltd) all cartoons;
Sebastian Quigley (Linden Artists) 6–15, 18–21, 28–29; Ian
Thompson 16–17, 22–25; Ross Watton (Garden Studio) 26–27.

FOR OWEN

Please note that in this book the term 'billion' equals
one thousand million (1,000,000,000).

# CONTENTS

# What is the universe?

The whole world and everything beyond is the universe. It is all the stars and planets, the Earth and its plants and animals, you and me – everything.

You are made of the same stuff as a star!

There are huge groups of stars in space. They are called galaxies, and they're like gigantic star-cities.

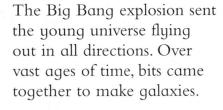

The Big Bang explosion sent the young universe flying out in all directions. Over vast ages of time, bits came together to make galaxies.

The galaxies are still speeding apart today, and the universe is getting bigger.

# When did it all begin?

Many astronomers think that everything in the universe was once packed together in one small lump. Then, about 14 billion years ago, there was a gigantic explosion of stuff that they call the Big Bang.

To see how the universe is getting bigger, watch the spots as you blow up a spotty balloon.

# Will the universe ever end?

Some astronomers think the universe will just carry on getting bigger as the galaxies speed apart. Others think that the galaxies may one day start falling back towards each other until they crash together in a Big Crunch!

Astronomers are scientists who study the stars and the planets.

No one knows where all the material to make the universe came from in the first place.

# What is the Milky Way?

The Milky Way is the galaxy we live in. It is made up of all the stars you can see in the sky at night, and lots and lots more you cannot see.

Astronomers usually give galaxies numbers instead of names. Only a few have names that tell us what they look like – the Whirlpool, the Sombrero, and the Black Eye, for example.

The Milky Way got its name because at night we can sometimes see part of it looking like a band of milky white light across the sky.

The Milky Way is a barred spiral galaxy. Below you can see what it looks like from above – a bit like a whirlpool with long, spiralling arms.

From the side, a spiral galaxy looks like two fried eggs stuck together.

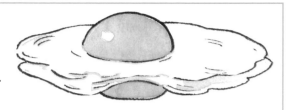

There are four main galaxy shapes. The barred spiral is one. Here are the others:

Irregular (no special shape)

We live on a planet called Earth, which travels around a star called the Sun.

Elliptical (egg-shaped)

Spiral

# How many stars are there?

There are about 1,000 billion stars in the Milky Way. That is nearly 200 stars for every person living on Earth today!

Although we cannot see all of it, astronomers have worked out how big the universe is and how many stars it has. There are about 100 billion billion stars, in around 100 billion galaxies. It is hard even to think about so many stars, let alone count them all!

# What are stars made of?

Sometimes, huge flame-like sheets of glowing gas shoot out from a star. These are called prominences.

Stars are not solid like the ground beneath your feet. Instead, they are made of gases like the air around you.

The two main gases in stars are called hydrogen and helium. They are the stars' fuel. Stars make heat and light from them.

Since ancient times, stargazers have seen patterns in the way stars are grouped in the sky. The patterns are called constellations.

The brightest star we can see in the night sky is called Sirius. Another name for it is the Dog Star. It is about twice as big as our Sun, but it gives out more than twenty times as much light!

# Why do stars twinkle?

Stars only twinkle when we look at them from Earth. Out in space their light shines steadily. We see them twinkling and shimmering because of the air around the Earth – as light from a star travels towards us, it is bent and wobbled by bubbles of hot and cold air.

Light bends when it passes through different things. If you put a straw in a glass of water, for example, it looks bent because it is half in air and half in water.

# Are stars star-shaped?

No, stars are round, like balls. We give them pointy edges when we draw them because this is what they look like from Earth, with their light blinking and twinkling.

# What is a red giant?

All stars are born, live for a very long time and then die. A red giant is a huge, ancient star.

Stars are being born all the time. They start their lives in star-nurseries called nebulas.

**1** All stars are born in huge, spinning clouds of gas and dust. Our Sun was born 4.6 billion years ago.

**3** Most stars are like our Sun and shine steadily for nearly all their lives.

**2** The gas and dust come together to make lots of balls, which become star clusters.

If you think of our Sun as shining like a car's headlights, then a red giant would shine like a lighthouse!

**4** Towards the end of their lives, stars like our Sun swell up and become as much as 100 times bigger. They turn into red giants. Our Sun will do this in about 5 billion years' time.

On Earth, a sugar-lump-sized piece of a white dwarf would weigh as much as a small car!

**5** When it has used up all its gas fuel, a red giant shrinks down into a white dwarf. It is then about 10,000 times smaller, but still very hot.

**6** The star cools down and ends its life billions of years later, as a black dwarf – a cold, black cinder.

Stars must have at least eight times as much gas fuel as our Sun to end their lives in supernova explosions.

# Which stars explode?

Different sorts of star lead different lives. Some stars have a lot more gas fuel in them than others. These really massive stars do not die quietly, by cooling down. Instead, they blow up in a great flash of light. Stars that explode like this are called supernovas.

11

# What is a black hole?

A black hole can happen when a massive star dies. The star falls in on itself, squashing all its material and becoming smaller and smaller. In the end all that is left is a place light cannot escape from − a black hole. Everything in space has a pulling force called gravity − galaxies, stars, planets like Earth, and even moons. Gravity holds things together and stops them floating off into space.

Earth's gravity keeps your feet on the ground. It pulls you down and stops you floating off into space.

When two large space bodies (such as a planet and a moon) get close enough, there is a pulling match between their forces of gravity. It is like a giant tug of war.

A planet's gravity holds its moons to it and stops them shooting off into space.

Stars that become black holes have really strong gravity − that is what pulls them inwards and makes them collapse.

Light is sucked into black holes in much the same way as water is sucked down a plug hole.

A star that gets too close to a black hole is sucked into it. Nothing, not even the star's light, can escape the pull of the black hole's gravity.

# How hot is the Sun?

Like all stars, our Sun is a huge ball of super-hot gas. It is hottest in the middle – the temperature there is around 15 million °C. The outside of the Sun is a lot cooler than the middle – only 6000°C. But this is still much, much hotter than the hottest kitchen oven!

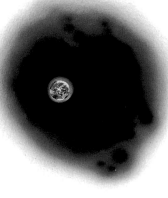

Dark patches called sunspots come and go on the face of the Sun. They make it look as though it has chickenpox. Sunspots are dark because they are cooler and so give out less light than the rest of the Sun.

Most sunspots are larger than the Earth.

Plants and animals could not live without the Sun's heat and light.

14

The Sun is the only star that is close enough to Earth for us to feel its heat. The next nearest star to Earth is called Proxima Centauri. Our Sun's light takes 8.3 minutes to reach us, but Proxima Centauri's takes 4.3 years!

The Sun uses more than 30 million truck loads of fuel every second!

# Will the Sun ever go out?

One day the Sun will use up all its gas fuel and die. But this will not happen in your lifetime, or your children's, or even your great-great-great grandchildren's! Astronomers think that the Sun has enough gas fuel to last for at least another 5 billion years.

# How many planets are there?

Our planet, the Earth, has seven neighbours. Together they make a family of eight main planets that travel around the Sun. We call the Sun, and all the space bodies that whirl around it, the solar system. Besides the Sun and the planets, the solar system includes moons, dwarf planets, asteroids and comets.

Comets are rather like huge, dirty snowballs. Most stay out on the edge of the solar system, but a few travel close to the Sun. These comets grow gas and dust tails, millions of kilometres long, when the Sun's heat starts to melt them.

The word planet comes from the Greek word *planetes*, which means wanderer.

Mars

Mercury    Venus    Earth    Jupiter

16

Planet

Orbit

Sun

An orbit is the path of a planet around the Sun, or a moon around a planet. The planets all have different orbits. Mercury is the closest to the Sun.

Millions of asteroids orbit the Sun, in a belt between Mars and Jupiter. Some are like grains of sand. Others are as big as houses. A few are the size of England!

# What is the difference between planets and stars?

The planets are not as big or as hot as stars, and they cannot make light of their own. They were made from the leftovers of the same gas and dust cloud that gave birth to our star, the Sun.

Saturn          Uranus                              Neptune

# Why is Earth so special?

Our planet is the only one in the
solar system with flowing, liquid
water and living things on it.
That makes it very special. It is the
third planet from the Sun, and it gets just
the right amount of heat and light to keep
us alive. Any closer, and it would
be too hot. Any farther
away, and it would
be too cold.

When the Sun turns into a red giant star, it will swallow up Mercury and get so large that it will cover half of our midday sky.

All planets spin as they orbit the Sun.

You can see what happens as the Earth spins if you turn a globe in the beam of light from a torch.

# Why does the Sun go out at night?

It gets dark at night because the Earth is spinning as it orbits the Sun. As parts of the Earth spin away from the Sun, they move out of its light into darkness. It takes a whole day and a night for the Earth to spin round once.

Astronomers think that millions of stars in the universe have families of planets. They have discovered more than 70 solar systems, and are finding more all the time.

# Which is the hottest planet?

Venus is not the closest planet to the Sun, but it is the hottest. The temperature there can reach 500°C – that is about 442 degrees hotter than the highest temperature ever recorded on Earth, at Al'Aziziyah in the Libyan desert, North Africa.

Although Mercury (right) is closer to the Sun, Venus is hotter! This is because Venus is covered by thick clouds of gas that act like a blanket, keeping in the Sun's heat.

Space probes have landed on Venus and sent back pictures and information to Earth. The probes were destroyed soon after landing, however, by the terrible climate on Venus.

Mars is the next planet from the Sun after ours, and people once thought that, like Earth, it might have living things. Space probes have been visiting, but they have not found any signs of life yet!

# Which is the red planet?

Mercury is covered in craters – hollows made by huge space rocks crashing into it.

If you could visit Mercury, you would see that the Sun looks more than twice as big there as it does from Earth. This is because Mercury is so much closer to the Sun.

Mars is often called the red planet. The ground there is covered in dusty red soil, which gets swept up by the wind to make pink clouds! The rocks on Mars have lots of iron in them, and iron goes red when it rusts. A better name for Mars might be the rusty planet!

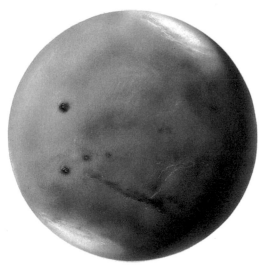

Living things need water. If there is any on Mars, it is frozen inside its north and south polar ice caps.

# Which is the biggest planet?

Jupiter is so huge that all the other planets could fit inside it! The beautiful patterns on its face are made by swirling clouds of gas, stirred up by powerful wind storms.

Planet Jupiter was named by the ancient Romans, after the king of their gods.

Jupiter is one of four planets with rings around them.

Great Red Spot

22

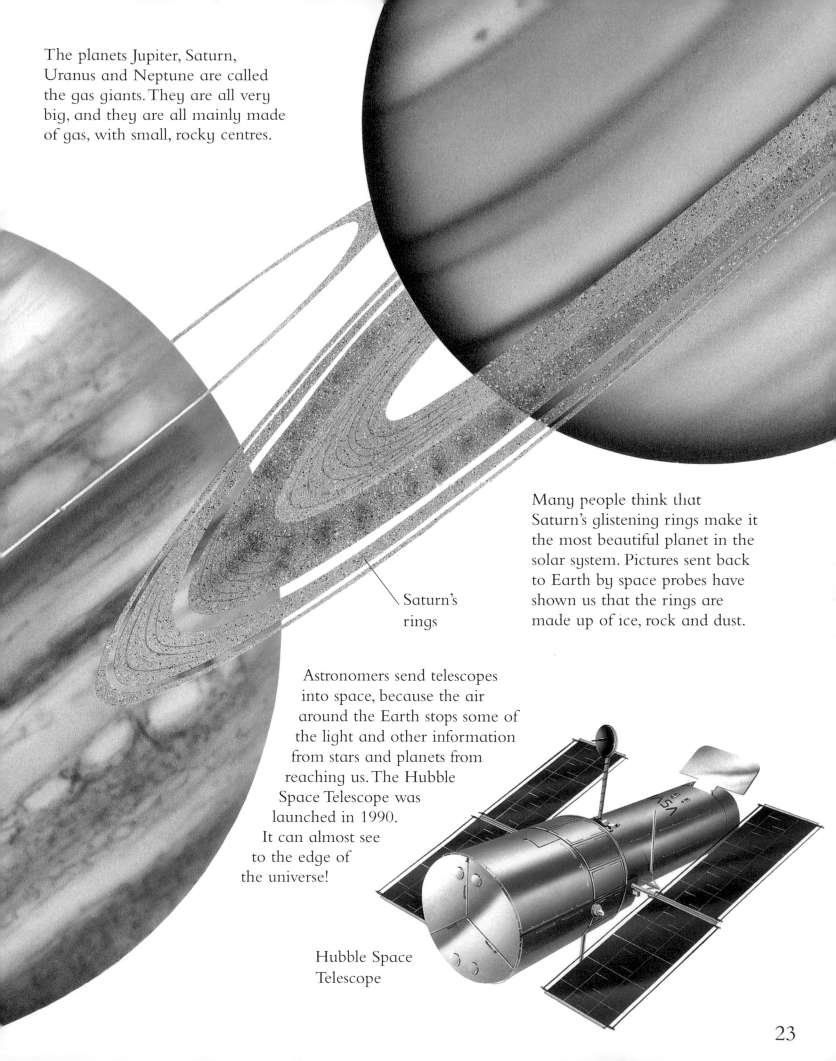

The planets Jupiter, Saturn, Uranus and Neptune are called the gas giants. They are all very big, and they are all mainly made of gas, with small, rocky centres.

Saturn's rings

Many people think that Saturn's glistening rings make it the most beautiful planet in the solar system. Pictures sent back to Earth by space probes have shown us that the rings are made up of ice, rock and dust.

Astronomers send telescopes into space, because the air around the Earth stops some of the light and other information from stars and planets from reaching us. The Hubble Space Telescope was launched in 1990. It can almost see to the edge of the universe!

Hubble Space Telescope

# Which planet is furthest from the Sun?

Neptune is the most distant and the coldest main planet. But beyond Neptune are at least a thousand icy rock bodies called Kuiper Belt Objects, as well as the 'dwarf planet' Pluto.

Pluto was discovered in 1930, and was named after the Roman god of the Underworld. It is now known as one of the solar system's dwarf planets.

On Neptune, the temperature is an incredibly icy –200°C. Even your ice cream would taste as hot as soup on this planet.

# Which planet is tipped over?

Uranus is the sideways planet. Its moons and rings go round its middle – but because it is on its side they look as if they circle it from top to toe. Uranus was not always like this. It got knocked over by a huge asteroid when it was young.

# How do we know about the furthest planets?

Until the American *Voyager 2* spacecraft visited Uranus in 1986 and Neptune in 1989, not a lot was known about these planets. *Voyager 2* gave us our first close-up look at these two distant worlds. The spacecraft's cameras showed us 16 of Uranus's moons and eight of Neptune's. Since then, more have been discovered using Earth's most powerful telescopes. Now we know that Neptune has 13 moons and Uranus has 27.

*Voyager 2* left Earth in 1977 and reached Neptune 12 years later, in 1989.

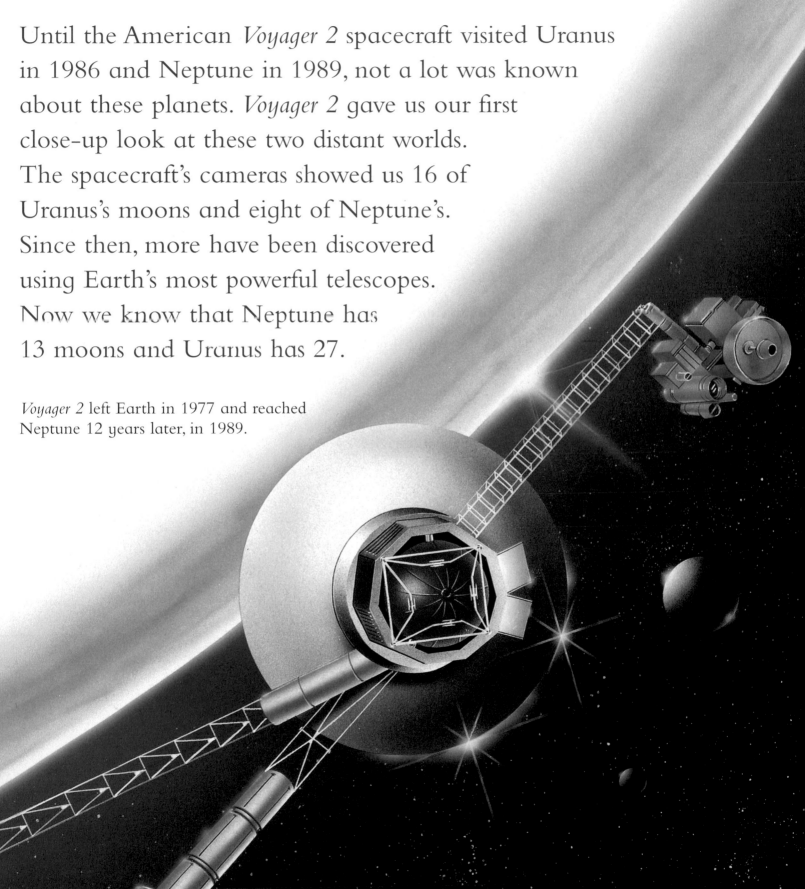

# Which planet has the biggest moons?

Ganymede

Io

Callisto

Our Moon

Moons are rocky bodies that orbit (circle) planets. Jupiter has at least 60 moons, and three of them, Ganymede, Callisto and Io – are larger than Earth's moon. Mercury and Venus are the only planets that do not have moons. All the other planets have at least one.

In pictures taken by the space probe *Voyager 2*, Io looks like a giant cheese and tomato pizza. The tomato colour comes from volcanoes.

# What is it like on our Moon?

Earth's Moon is dry, dusty and lifeless. There is no air to breathe or water to drink. During the day it is so hot that your blood would boil. At night it is freezing cold – not a good place to take a holiday!

# Which planet's moons look like potatoes?

Mars has two tiny moons, which look like lumpy old potatoes. They are called Deimos and Phobos and, unlike larger moons, they are not round.

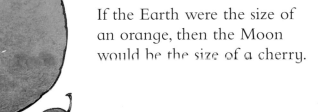

If the Earth were the size of an orange, then the Moon would be the size of a cherry.

On 20 July 1969, two American astronauts became the first living things ever to set foot on the Moon. Their names were Neil Armstrong and Buzz Aldrin, and their space mission was called *Apollo 11*.

The Moon's gravity is weaker than Earth's. You would be much lighter on the Moon – only a sixth of your Earth-weight. So you would be able to jump six times as high!

# How fast do space rockets go?

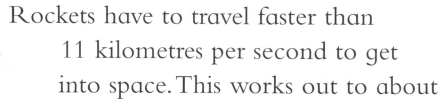

Rockets have to travel faster than
11 kilometres per second to get
into space. This works out to about
40,000 kilometres per hour – and car drivers can
get into trouble for speeding at 120 kilometres per hour!
If rockets did not travel so fast they would not be able to
escape the enormously strong pull of Earth's gravity.

*Saturn V*

The tallest rocket ever launched
was the *Saturn V* that took the
*Apollo 11* spacecraft into space,
and the first people to the Moon.
It was more than 100m tall.

**Space Shuttle**

*Ariane 4*

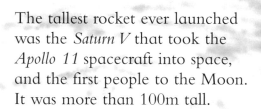

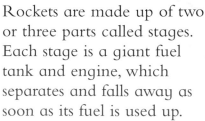

Rockets are made up of two
or three parts called stages.
Each stage is a giant fuel
tank and engine, which
separates and falls away as
soon as its fuel is used up.

At the top of the rocket is its payload – a satellite, a robotic space probe, or a spacecraft carrying astronauts.

Satellites can be used by one country to spy on another.

# What are rockets used for?

Rockets are mainly used to put machines called satellites into orbit around the Earth. Different sorts of satellite are launched to do many different jobs.

Communications satellites pick up and send on TV and telephone signals.

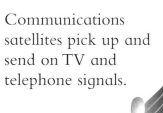

Navigation satellites help ships and aircraft to find their way.

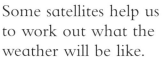

Satellite photographs and maps help scientists to study the Earth and what it is made of.

Some satellites help us to work out what the weather will be like.

# Why do astronauts wear space suits?

There is no air to breathe in space and, depending on whether a spacecraft is in or out of the Sun's light, it's either very hot or very cold. Without space suits to protect them outside their spacecraft, astronauts would die.

Astronauts sleep in bags which are strapped down to stop them floating about. Astronauts even have to tuck or tie their arms in to stop them waving about!

Astronauts have to wear seatbelts to stop them floating away when they use the toilet. Space toilets do not flush. Everything is sucked away instead.

Space stretches you – astronauts can come back as much as 5 centimetres taller!

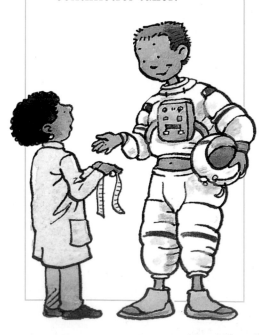

# Why do astronauts float in space?

Gravity is everywhere. But astronauts on a spacecraft orbiting Earth do not experience it in the same way. The craft and astronauts are further away from the pull of Earth's gravity, so they are actually 'falling around' the Earth rather than down towards it.

The gold visors on their helmets protect the astronauts' eyes from the Sun's harmful rays.

When they go on 'spacewalks' outside a spacecraft or space station, astronauts work in pairs. One may be safely harnessed to a robotic arm (above), while another works nearby. On their backs they wear a life-support unit. This provides oxygen for the astronauts to breathe, and pumps cooled liquid around their space suits to keep them at the right temperature.

# Index

## A
Aldrin, Buzz 27
*Apollo 11* 27
Armstrong, Neil 27
asteroids 16, 17
astronauts 27, 29, 30–31
astronomers 23, 25

## B
Big Bang 4
Big Crunch 5
black dwarves 11
black holes 12–13

## C
Callisto 26
comets 16–17
constellations 8
craters 21

## D
Dog Star *see* Sirius
dwarf planets 24

## E
Earth 4, 6, 12, 15, 16, 18–19, 20, 20, 27, 29
elliptical galaxies 7

## G
galaxies 4, 5, 6–7
Ganymede 26
gas giants (planets) 23
gravity 12, 27, 28, 30
Great Red Spot 22

## H
helium 8
Hubble Space Telescope 23
hydrogen 8

## I
Io 26
irregular galaxies 7

## J
Jupiter 16, 22–23, 26

## L
life forms 14, 18, 21

## M
Mars 16, 21, 27
Mercury 16, 19, 20, 21, 26
Milky Way 6–7
Moon (Earth's) 26–27
moons 12, 16, 25, 26–27

## N
nebulas 10
Neptune 17, 23, 24, 25

## O
orbits 17, 19, 24, 29

## P
payloads 29
planets 12, 16–23
Pluto 17, 24
prominences 8
Proxima Centauri 15

## R
red giants 10, 11, 19
rings 23
rockets 28–29

## S
satellites 29
Saturn 17, 23
*Saturn V* rocket 28
Sirius 8
solar systems 16–27
spacecraft 25, 28–29, 30–31
space probes 21, 29
space rockets 28–29
space shuttles 28
space suits 30
spiral galaxies 6, 7
star clusters 10
stars 4–15, 17
    composition 8–9
    life and death 10–11
    *see also* Sun
starlight 9, 12, 13
Sun 10, 11, 14–15, 16, 17, 18, 19, 25
sunspots 14
supernovas 11

## T
telescopes 23, 25
toilets, space 30

## U
universe 4–5, 7, 23
Uranus 17, 23, 24, 25

## V
Venus 16, 20, 26
*Voyager 2* 25

## W
white dwarves 11

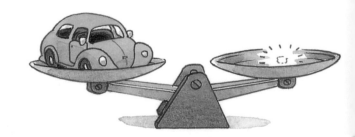